O9-BSU-780

THE WORLD'S ONE THOUSAND BEST POEMS

VOLUME TEN

WIDDEMER-ZOLA

THE WORLD'S ONE THOUSAND BEST POEMS

(IN TEN VOLUMES)

BERTON BRALEY
EDITOR-IN-CHIEF

VOLUME TEN

WIDDEMER-ZOLA

(Complete Index)

FUNK & WAGNALLS COMPANY
NEW YORK AND LONDON

Acknowledgments of individual copyrights will be found in this volume

TABLE OF CONTENTS

VOLUME X

TABLE OF CONTENTS

THE WORLD'S ONE THOUSAND BEST POEMS

VOLUME TEN

THE WORLD'S 1000 BEST POEMS

MARGARET WIDDEMER

THE MODERN WOMAN TO HER LOVER

I SHALL not lie to you any more,
  Flatter or fawn to attain my end—
I am what never has been before,
  Woman—and Friend.

I shall be strong as a man is strong,
  I shall be fair as a man is fair,
Hand in locked hand we shall pass along
  To a purer air.

I shall not drag at your bridle-rein,
  Knee pressed to knee we shall ride the hill:
I shall not lie to you ever again—
  Will you love me still?

FACTORIES

I HAVE shut my little sister in from life and light
  (For a rose, for a ribbon, for a wreath across my hair)
I have made her restless feet still until the night,
  Locked from sweets of summer and from wild spring air;

I who ranged the meadowlands, free from sun to sun,
Free to sing and pull the buds and watch the far wings fly,
I have bound my sister till her playing time was done—
Oh, my little sister, was it I? Was it I?

I have robbed my sister of her day of maidenhood
(For a robe, for a feather, for a trinket's restless spark)
Shut from love till dusk shall fall, how shall she know good,
How shall she go scatheless through the sin-lit dark?
I who could be innocent, I who could be gay,
I who could have love and mirth before the light went by,
I have put my sister in her mating-time away—
Sister, my young sister, was it I? Was it I?

I have robbed my sister of the lips against her breast,
(For a coin, for the weaving of my children's lace and lawn)
Feet that pace beside the loom, hands that cannot rest—
How can she know motherhood, whose strength is gone?
I who took no heed of her, starved and labor-worn,
I, against whose placid heart my sleepy gold-heads lie,
Round my path they cry to me, little souls unborn—
God of Life! Creator! It was I! It was I!

ELLA WHEELER WILCOX

1855—1919

THE DUET

I WAS smoking a cigarette;
Maud, my wife, and the tenor McKey,
Were singing together a blithe duet,
And days it were better I should forget
  Came suddenly back to me.
Days when life seemed a gay masque ball,
And to love and be loved was the sum of it all.

As they sang together, the whole scene fled,
The room's rich hangings, the sweet home air,
Stately Maud, with her proud blonde head,
And I seemed to see in her place instead
  A wealth of blue-black hair,
And a face, ah! your face,—yours, Lisette,
A face it were wiser I should forget.

We were back—well, no matter when or where,
But you remember, I know, Lisette,
I saw you, dainty, and debonnaire,
With the very same look that you used to wear
  In the days I should forget.
And your lips, as red as the vintage we quaffed,
Were pearl-edged bumpers of wine when you
    laughed.

Two small slippers with big rosettes,
Peeped out under your kilt-skirt there,
While we sat smoking our cigarettes
(Oh, I shall be dust when my heart forgets!)

And singing that selfsame air;
And between the verses for interlude,
I kissed your throat, and your shoulders nude.

You were so full of a subtle fire,
You were so warm and so sweet, Lisette;
You were everything men admire
And there were no fetters to make us tire,
For you were—a pretty grisette.
But you loved, as only such natures can,
With a love that makes heaven or hell for a man.

* * * * * *

They have ceased singing that old duet,
Stately Maud and the tenor McKey.
"You are burning your coat with your cigarette,
And qu' avez vous, dearest, your lids are wet,"
Maud says, as she leans o'er me,
And I smile, and lie to her, husband-wise,
"Oh, it is nothing but smoke in my eyes."

LAUGH, AND THE WORLD LAUGHS WITH YOU

Laugh, and the world laughs with you;
Weep, and you weep alone;
For this brave old earth must borrow its mirth,
It has trouble enough of its own.
Sing, and the hills will answer;
Sigh! it is lost on the air;
The echoes bound to a joyful sound,
But shrink from voicing care.

Rejoice, and men will seek you;
  Grieve, and they turn and go;
They want full measure of all your pleasure,
  But they do not want your woe.
Be glad, and your friends are many;
  Be sad, and you lose them all—
There are none to decline your nectared wine,
  But alone you must drink life's gall.

Feast, and your halls are crowded;
  Fast, and the world goes by.
Succeed and give, and it helps you live,
  But no man can help you die.
There is room in the halls of pleasure
  For a long and lordly train:
But one by one we must all file on
  Through the narrow aisles of pain.

OSCAR WILDE

1856—1900

HELAS!

To drift with every passion till my soul
Is a stringed lute on which all winds can play,
Is it for this that I have given away
Mine ancient wisdom, and austere control?
Methinks my life is a twice-written scroll
Scrawled over on some boyish holiday
With idle songs for pipe and virelay,
Which do but mar the secret of the whole.
Surely there was a time I might have trod
The sunlit heights, and from life's dissonance

Struck one clear chord to reach the ears of God:
Is that time dead? lo! with a little rod
I did but touch the honey of romance—
And must I lose a soul's inheritance?

FROM "THE BALLAD OF READING GAOL"

I

HE did not wear his scarlet coat,
  For blood and wine are red,
And blood and wine were on his hands
  When they found him with the dead,
The poor dead woman whom he loved,
  And murdered in her bed.

He walked amongst the Trial Men
  In a suit of shabby grey;
A cricket cap was on his head,
  And his step seemed light and gay;
But I never saw a man who looked
  So wistfully at the day.

I never saw a man who looked
  With such a wistful eye
Upon that little tent of blue
  Which prisoners call the sky,
And at every drifting cloud that went
  With sails of silver by.

I walked, with other souls in pain,
  Within another ring,
And was wondering if the man had done
  A great or little thing,
When a voice behind me whispered low,
  "That fellow's got to swing."

Dear Christ! the very prison walls
  Suddenly seemed to reel,
And the sky above my head became
  Like a casque of scorching steel;
And, though I was a soul in pain,
  My pain I could not feel.

I only knew what hunted thought
  Quickened his step, and why
He looked upon the garish day
  With such a wistful eye;
The man had killed the thing he loved,
  And so he had to die.

* * * * * *

Yet each man kills the thing he loves,
  By each let this be heard,
Some do it with a bitter look,
  Some with a flattering word,
The coward does it with a kiss,
  The brave man with a sword!

Some kill their love when they are young,
  And some when they are old;
Some strangle with the hands of Lust,
  Some with the hands of Gold:
The kindest use a knife, because
  The dead so soon grow cold.

Some love too little, some too long,
  Some sell, and others buy;
Some do the deed with many tears,
  And some without a sigh:
For each man kills the thing he loves,
  Yet each man does not die.

He does not die a death of shame
  On a day of dark disgrace,
Nor have a noose about his neck,
  Nor a cloth upon his face,
Nor drop feet foremost through the floor
  Into an empty space.

* * * * * *

He does not sit with silent men
  Who watch him night and day;
Who watch him when he tries to weep,
  And when he tries to pray;
Who watch him lest himself should rob
  The prison of its prey.

He does not wake at dawn to see
  Dread figures throng his room,
The shivering Chaplain robed in white,
  The Sheriff stern with gloom,
And the Governor all in shiny black,
  With the yellow face of Doom.

He does not rise in piteous haste
  To put on convict-clothes,
While some coarse-mouthed Doctor gloats, and notes
  Each new and nerve-twitched pose,
Fingering a watch whose little ticks
  Are like horrible hammer-blows.

He does not know that sickening thirst
  That sands one's throat, before
The hangman with his gardener's gloves
  Slips through the padded door,
And binds one with three leathern thongs,
  That the throat may thirst no more.

He does not bend his head to hear
  The Burial Office read,
Nor, while the terror of his soul
  Tells him he is not dead,
Cross his own coffin, as he moves
  Into the hideous shed.

He does not stare upon the air
  Through a little roof of glass:
He does not pray with lips of clay
  For his agony to pass;
Nor feel upon his shuddering cheek
  The kiss of Caiaphas.

II

Six weeks our guardsman walked the yard,
  In the suit of shabby grey:
His cricket cap was on his head,
  And his step seemed light and gay,
But I never saw a man who looked
  So wistfully at the day.

I never saw a man who looked
  With such a wistful eye
Upon that little tent of blue
  Which prisoners call the sky,
And at every wandering cloud that trailed
  Its ravelled fleeces by,

He did not wring his hands, as do
  Those witless men who dare
To try to rear the changeling Hope
  In the cave of black Despair:
He only looked upon the sun,
  And drank the morning air.

He did not wring his hands nor weep,
  Nor did he peek or pine,
But he drank the air as though it held
  Some healthful anodyne;
With open mouth he drank the sun
  As though it had been wine!

And I and all the souls in pain,
  Who tramped the other ring,
Forgot if we ourselves had done
  A great or little thing,
And watched with gaze of dull amaze
  The man who had to swing.

And strange it was to see him pass
  With a step so light and gay,
And strange it was to see him look
  So wistfully at the day,
And strange it was to think that he
  Had such a debt to pay.

* * * * * *

For oak and elm have pleasant leaves
  That in the spring-time shoot:
But grim to see is the gallows-tree,
  With its adder-bitten root,
And, green or dry, a man must die
  Before it bears its fruit!

The loftiest place is that seat of grace
  For which all worldlings try:
But who would stand in hempen band
  Upon a scaffold high,
And through a murderer's collar take
  His last look at the sky?

It is sweet to dance to violins
  When Love and Life are fair:
To dance to flutes, to dance to lutes
  Is delicate and rare:
But it is not sweet with nimble feet
  To dance upon the air!

So with curious eyes and sick surmise
  We watched him day by day,
And wondered if each one of us
  Would end the self-same way,
For none can tell to what red Hell
  His sightless soul may stray.

At last the dead man walked no more
  Amongst the Trial Men,
And I knew that he was standing up
  In the black dock's dreadful pen,
And that never would I see his face
  In God's sweet world again.

Like two doomed ships that pass in storm
  We had crossed each other's way:
But we made no sign, we said no word,
  We had no word to say;
For we did not meet in the holy night,
  But in the shameful day.

A prison wall was round us both,
  Two outcast men we were:
The world had thrust us from its heart,
  And God from out His care:
And the iron gin that waits for Sin
  Had caught us in its snare.

There is no chapel on the day
  On which they hang a man:
The Chaplain's heart is far too sick,
  Or his face is far too wan,
Or there is that written in his eyes
  Which none should look upon.

So they kept us close till nigh on noon,
  And then they rang the bell,
And the Warders with their jingling keys
  Opened each listening cell,
And down the iron stair we tramped,
  Each from his separate Hell.

Out into God's sweet air we went,
  But not in wonted way,
For this man's face was white with fear,
  And that man's face was grey,
And I never saw sad men who looked
  So wistfully at the day.

I never saw sad men who looked
  With such a wistful eye
Upon that little tent of blue
  We prisoners called the sky,
And at every careless cloud that passed
  In happy freedom by.

But there were those amongst us all
  Who walked with downcast head,
And knew that, had each got his due,
  They should have died instead:
He had but killed a thing that lived,
  Whilst they had killed the dead.

For he who sins a second time
  Wakes a dead soul to pain,
And draws it from its spotted shroud,
  And makes it bleed again,
And makes it bleed great gouts of blood,
  And makes it bleed in vain!

* * * * * *

Like ape or clown, in monstrous garb
  With crooked arrows starred,
Silently we went round and round,
  The slippery asphalte yard;
Silently we went round and round
  And no man spoke a word.

Silently we went round and round,
  And through each hollow mind
The Memory of dreadful things
  Rushed like a dreadful wind,
And Horror stalked before each man,
  And Terror crept behind.

The Warders strutted up and down,
  And kept their herd of brutes,
Their uniforms were spick and span,
  And they wore their Sunday suits,
But we knew the work they had been at,
  By the quicklime on their boots.

For where a grave had opened wide,
  There was no grave at all:
Only a stretch of mud and sand
  By the hideous prison-wall,
And a little heap of burning lime,
  That the man should have his pall.

For he has a pall, this wretched man,
  Such as few men can claim:
Deep down below a prison-yard,
  Naked for greater shame,
He lies, with fetters on each foot,
  Wrapt in a sheet of flame!

And all the while the burning lime
  Eats flesh and bone away,
It eats the brittle bone by night,
  And the soft flesh by day,
It eats the flesh and bone by turns,
  But it eats the heart alway.

* * * * * *

I know not whether Laws be right,
  Or whether Laws be wrong;
All that we know who lie in gaol
  Is that the wall is strong;
And that each day is like a year,
  A year whose days are long.

But this I know; that every Law
  That men have made for Man,
Since first Man took his brother's life,
  And the sad world began,
But straws the wheat and saves the chaff
  With a most evil fan.

This too I know—and wise it were
  If each could know the same—
That every prison that men build
  Is built with bricks of shame,
And bound with bars lest Christ should see
  How men their brothers maim.

With bars they blur the gracious moon,
  And blind the goodly sun:
And they do well to hide their Hell,
  For in it things are done
That son of God nor son of Man
  Ever should look upon!

* * * * * *

In Reading gaol by Reading town
  There is a pit of shame,
And in it lies a wretched man
  Eaten by teeth of flame,
In a burning winding-sheet he lies,
  And his grave has got no name.

And there, till Christ call forth the dead,
  In silence let him lie:
No need to waste the foolish tear,
  Or heave the windy sigh:
The man had killed the thing he loved,
  And so he had to die.

And all men kill the thing they love,
  By all let this be heard,
Some do it with a bitter look,
  Some with a flattering word,
The coward does it with a kiss,
  The brave man with a sword!

FLOWER OF LOVE

Sweet, I blame you not, for mine the fault was, had
    I not been made of common clay
I had climbed the higher heights unclimbed yet,
    seen the fuller air, the larger day.

From the wildness of my wasted passion I had struck
a better, clearer song,
Lit some lighter light of freer freedom, battled with
some Hydra-headed wrong.

Had my lips been smitten into music by the kisses
that made them bleed,
You had walked with Bice and the angels on that
verdant and enamelled mead.

I had trod the road which Dante treading saw the
sun of seven circles shine,
Ay! Perchance had seen the heavens opening, as
they opened to the Florentine.

And the mighty nations would have crowned me,
who am crownless now and without name,
And some orient dawn had found me kneeling on
the threshold of the House of Fame.

I had sat within that marble circle where the oldest
bard is as the young,
And the pipe is ever dropping honey, and the lyre's
strings are ever strung.

Keats had lifted up his hymeneal curls from out the
poppy-seeded wine,
With ambrosial mouth had kissed my forehead,
clasped the hand of noble love in mine.

And at springtide, when the apple-blossoms brush the
burnished bosom of the dove,
Two young lovers lying in an orchard would have
read the story of our love.

Would have read the legend of my passion, known
the bitter secret of my heart,
Kissed as we have kissed, but never parted as we
two are fated now to part.

For the crimson flower of our life is eaten by the
canker-worm of truth,
And no hand can gather up the fallen withered petals
of the rose of youth.

Yet I am not sorry that I loved you—ah! what else
had I a boy to do,—
For the hungry teeth of time devour, and the silent-
footed years pursue.

Rudderless, we drift athwart a tempest, and when
once the storm of youth is past,
Without lyre, without lute or chorus, Death the
silent pilot comes at last.

And within the grave there is no pleasure, for the
blindworm battens on the root,
And Desire shudders into ashes, and the tree of
Passion bears no fruit.

Ah! what else had I to do but love you, God's own
mother was less dear to me,
And less dear the Cytheræan rising like an argent lily
from the sea.

I have made my choice, have lived my poems, and,
though youth is gone in wasted days,
I have found the lover's crown of myrtle better than
the poet's crown of bays.

THE SPHINX

IN a dim corner of my room for longer than my fancy thinks
A beautiful and silent Sphinx has watched me through the shifting gloom.

Inviolate and immobile she does not rise, she does not stir
For silver moons are naught to her and naught to her the suns that reel.

Red follows grey across the air, the waves of moonlight ebb and flow
But with the Dawn she does not go and in the night-time she is there.

Dawn follows Dawn and Nights grow old and all the while this curious cat
Lies couching on the Chinese mat with eyes of satin rimmed with gold.

Upon the mat she lies and leers and on the tawny throat of her
Flutters the soft and silky fur or ripples to her pointed ears.

Come forth, my lovely seneschal! so somnolent, so statuesque!
Come forth you exquisite grotesque! half woman and half animal!

Come forth my lovely languorous Sphinx! and put your head upon my knee!
And let me stroke your throat and see your body spotted like the Lynx!

And let me touch those curving claws of yellow ivory and grasp
The tail that like a monstrous Asp coils round your heavy velvet paws!

A thousand weary centuries are thine while I have hardly seen
Some twenty summers cast their green for Autumn's gaudy liveries.

But you can read the Hieroglyphs on the great sandstone obelisks,
And you have talked with Basilisks, and you have looked on Hippogriffs.

O tell me, were you standing by when Isis to Osiris knelt?
And did you watch the Egyptian melt her union for Antony

And drink the jewel-drunken wine and bend her head in mimic awe
To see the huge proconsul draw the salted tunny from the brine?

And did you mark the Cyprian kiss white Adon on his catafalque?
And did you follow Amenalk, the God of Heliopolis?

And did you talk with Thoth, and did you hear the moon-horned Io weep?
And know the painted kings who sleep beneath the wedge-shaped Pyramid?

Lift up your large black satin eyes which are like cushions where one sinks!
Fawn at my feet, fantastic Sphinx! and sing me all your memories!

Sing to me of the Jewish maid who wandered with the Holy Child,
And how you led them through the wild, and how they slept beneath your shade.

Sing to me of that odorous green eve when couching by the marge
You heard from Adrian's gilded barge the laughter of Antinous

And lapped the stream and fed your drouth and watched with hot and hungry stare
The ivory body of that rare young slave with his pomegranate mouth!

Sing to me of the Labyrinth in which the twy-formed bull was stalled!
Sing to me of the night you crawled across the temple's granite plinth

When through the purple corridors the screaming scarlet Ibis flew
In terror, and a horrid dew dripped from the moaning Mandragores,

And the great torpid crocodile within the tank shed slimy tears,
And tare the jewels from his ears and staggered back into the Nile,

And the priests cursed you with shrill psalms as in
your claws you seized their snake
And crept away with it to slake your passion by the
shuddering palms.

Who were your lovers? who were they who wrestled
for you in the dust?
Which was the vessel of your Lust? What Leman
had you, every day?

Did giant Lizards come and crouch before you on
the reedy banks?
Did Gryphons with great metal flanks leap on you
in your trampled couch?

Did monstrous hippopotami come sidling toward you
in the mist?
Did gilt-scaled dragons writhe and twist with passion as you passed them by?

And from the brick-built Lycian tomb what horrible
Chimera came
With fearful heads and fearful flame to breed new
wonders from your womb?

Or had you shameful secret quests and did you
hurry to your home
Some Nereid coiled in amber foam with curious rock
crystal breasts?

Or did you treading through the froth call to the
brown Sidonian
For tidings of Leviathan, Leviathan or Behemoth?

Or did you when the sun was set climb up the cactus-covered slope
To meet your swarthy Ethiop whose body was of polished jet?

Or did you while the earthen skiffs dropped down the grey Nilotic flats
At twilight and the flickering bats flew round the temple's triple glyphs

Steal to the border of the bar and swim across the silent lake
And slink into the vault and make the Pyramid your lúpanar

Till from each black sarcophagus rose up the painted swathèd dead?
Or did you lure unto your bed the ivory-horned Tragelaphos?

Or did you love the god of flies who plagued the Hebrews and was splashed
With wine unto the waist? or Pasht, who had green beryls for her eyes?

Or that young god, the Tyrian, who was more amorous than the dove
Of Ashtaroth? or did you love the god of the Assyrian

Whose wings, like strange transparent talc, rose high above his hawk-faced head,
Painted with silver and with red and ribbed with rods of Oreichalch?

Or did huge Apis from his car leap down and lay before your feet
Big blossoms of the honey-sweet and honey-coloured nenuphar?

How subtle-secret is your smile! Did you love none then? Nay, I know
Great Ammon was your bedfellow! He lay with you beside the Nile!

The river-horses in the slime trumpeted when they saw him come
Odorous with Syrian galbanum and smeared with spikenard and with thyme.

He came along the river bank like some tall galley argent-sailed,
He strode across the waters, mailed in beauty, and the waters sank.

He strode across the desert sand: he reached the valley where you lay:
He waited till the dawn of day: then touched your black breasts with his hand.

You kissed his mouth with mouths of flame: you made the hornèd god your own:
You stood behind him on his throne: you called him by his secret name.

You whispered monstrous oracles into the caverns of his ears:
With blood of goats and blood of steers you taught him monstrous miracles.

White Ammon was your bedfellow! Your chamber was the steaming Nile!
And with your curved archaic smile you watched his passion come and go

---

With Syrian oils his brows were bright: and wide-spread as a tent at noon
His marble limbs made pale the moon and lent the day a larger light.

His long hair was nine cubits' span and coloured like that yellow gem
Which hidden in their garment's hem the merchants bring from Kurdistan.

His face was as the must that lies upon a vat of new-made wine:
The seas could not insapphirine the perfect azure of his eyes.

His thick soft throat was white as milk and threaded with the veins of blue:
And curious pearls like frozen dew were broidered on his flowing silk.

On pearl and porphyry pedestalled he was too bright to look upon:
For on his ivory breast there shone the wondrous ocean-emerald,

That mystic moonlit jewel which some diver of the Colchian caves
Had found beneath the blackening waves and carried to the Colchian witch.

Before his gilded galiot ran naked vine-wreathed corybants,
And lines of swaying elephants knelt down to draw his chariot,

And lines of swarthy Nubians bare up his litter as he rode
Down the great granite-paven road between the nodding peacock-fans.

The merchants brought him steatite from Sidon in their painted ships:
The meanest cup that touched his lips was fashioned from a chrysolite.

The merchants brought him cedar chests of rich apparel bound with cords:
His train was borne by Memphian lords: young kings were glad to be his guests.

Ten hundred shaven priests did bow to Ammon's altar day and night,
Ten hundred lamps did wave their light through Ammon's carven house—and now

Foul snake and speckled adder with their young ones crawl from stone to stone
For ruined is the house and prone the great rose-marble monolith!

Wild ass or trotting jackal comes and couches in the mouldering gates:
Wild satyrs call unto their mates across the fallen fluted drums.

And on the summit of the pilc the blue-faced ape
of Horus sits
And gibbers while the fig-tree splits the pillars of the
peristyle.

The god is scattered here and there: deep hidden in
the windy sand
I saw his giant granite hand still clenched in im-
potent despair.

And many a wandering caravan of stately negroes
silken-shawled,
Crossing the desert, halts appalled before the neck
that none can span.

And many a bearded Bedouin draws back his yellow-
striped burnous
To gaze upon the Titan thews of him who was thy
paladin.

Go, seek his fragments on the moor and wash them
in the evening dew,
And from their pieces make anew thy mutilated
paramour!

Go, seek them where they lie alone and from their
broken pieces make
Thy bruisèd bedfellow! And wake mad passion in
the senseless stone!

Charm his dull ear with Syrian hymns! he loved
your body! oh, be kind,
Pour spikenard on his hair, and wind soft rolls of
linen round his limbs!

Wind round his head the figured coins! stain with red fruits those pallid lips!
Weave purple for his shrunken hips! and purple for his barren loins!

Away to Egypt! Have no fear. Only one God has ever died.
Only one God has let His side be wounded by a soldier's spear.

But these, thy lovers, are not dead. Still by the hundred-cubit gate
Dog-faced Anubis sits in state with lotus-lilies for thy head.

Still from his chair of porphyry gaunt Memnon strains his lidless eyes
Across the empty land, and cries each yellow morning unto thee.

And Nilus with his broken horn lies in his black and oozy bed
And till thy coming will not spread his waters on the withering corn.

Your lovers are not dead, I know. They will rise up and hear your voice
And clash their cymbals and rejoice and run to kiss your mouth! And so,

Set wings upon your argosies! Set horses to your ebon car!
Back to your Nile! Or if you are grown sick of dead divinities

Follow some roving lion's spoor across the copper-
coloured plain,
Reach out and hale him by the mane and bid him
be your paramour!

Couch by his side upon the grass and set your white
teeth in his throat
And when you hear his dying note lash your long
flanks of polished brass

And take a tiger for your mate, whose amber sides
are flecked with black,
And ride upon his gilded back in triumph through
the Theban gate,

And toy with him in amorous jests, and when he
turns, and snarls, and gnaws,
O smite him with your jasper claws! and bruise him
with your agate breasts!

Why are you tarrying? Get hence! I weary of your
sullen ways,
I weary of your steadfast gaze, your somnolent
magnificence.

Your horrible and heavy breath makes the light
flicker in the lamp,
And on my brow I feel the damp and dreadful dews
of night and death.

Your eyes are like fantastic moons that shiver in
some stagnant lake,
Your tongue is like a scarlet snake that dances to
fantastic tunes,

Your pulse makes poisonous melodies, and your black throat is like the hole
Left by some torch or burning coal on Saracenic tapestries.

Away! The sulphur-coloured stars are hurrying through the Western gate!
Away! Or it may be too late to climb their silent silver cars!

See, the dawn shivers round the grey gilt-dialled towers, and the rain
Streams down each diamonded pane and blurs with tears the wannish day.

What snake-tressed fury fresh from Hell, with uncouth gestures and unclean,
Stole from the poppy-drowsy queen and led you to a student's cell?

What songless tongueless ghost of sin crept through the curtains of the night,
And saw my taper burning bright, and knocked, and bade you enter in.

Are there not others more accursed, whiter with leprosies than I?
Are Abana and Pharphar dry that you come here to slake your thirst?

Get hence, you loathsome mystery! Hideous animal, get hence!
You wake in me each bestial sense, you make me what I would not be.

You make my creed a barren sham, you wake foul dreams of sensual life,
And Atys with his blood-stained knife were better than the thing I am.

False Sphinx! False Sphinx! By reedy Styx old Charon, leaning on his oar,
Waits for my coin. Go thou before, and leave me to my crucifix,

Whose pallid burden, sick with pain, watches the world with wearied eyes,
And weeps for every soul that dies, and weeps for every soul in vain.

TO MY WIFE

WITH A COPY OF MY POEMS

I can write no stately proem
As a prelude to my lay;
From a poet to a poem
I would dare to say.

For if of these fallen petals
One to you seem fair,
Love will waft it till it settles
On your hair.

And when wind and winter harden
All the loveless land,
It will whisper of the garden,
You will understand.

REQUIESCAT

Tread lightly, she is near
  Under the snow,
Speak gently, she can hear
  The daisies grow.

All her bright golden hair
  Tarnished with rust,
She that was young and fair
  Fallen to dust.

Lily-like, white as snow,
  She hardly knew
She was a woman, so
  Sweetly she grew.

Coffin-board, heavy stone,
  Lie on her breast,
I vex my heart alone,
  She is at rest.

Peace, Peace, she cannot hear
  Lyre or sonnet,
All my life's buried here,
  Heap earth upon it.

LA BELLA DONNA DELLA MIA MENTE

My limbs are wasted with a flame,
  My feet are sore with travelling,
For, calling on my Lady's name,
  My lips have now forgot to sing.

O Linnet in the wild-rose brake
  Strain for my Love thy melody,
O Lark sing louder for love's sake,
  My gentle Lady passeth by.

O almond-blossoms bend adown
  Until ye reach her drooping head;
O twining branches weave a crown
  Of apple-blossoms white and red.

She is too fair for any man
  To see or hold his heart's delight,
Fairer than Queen or courtesan
  Or moon-lit water in the night.

Her hair is bound with myrtle leaves,
  (Green leaves upon her golden hair!)
Green grasses through the yellow sheaves
  Of autumn corn are not more fair.

EMMA HART WILLARD

1787—1870

ROCKED IN THE CRADLE OF THE DEEP

Rocked in the cradle of the deep
I lay me down in peace to sleep;
Secure I rest upon the wave,
For thou, O Lord! hast power to save.
I know thou wilt not slight my call,
For Thou dost mark the sparrow's fall;
And calm and peaceful shall I sleep,
Rocked in the cradle of the deep.

When in the dead of night I lie
And gaze upon the trackless sky,
The star-bespangled heavenly scroll,
The boundless waters as they roll,—
I feel thy wondrous power to save
From perils of the stormy wave:
Rocked in the cradle of the deep,
I calmly rest and soundly sleep.

And such the trust that still were mine,
Though stormy winds swept o'er the brine,
Or though the tempest's fiery breath
Roused me from sleep to wreck and death.
In ocean cave, still safe with Thee
The germ of immortality!
And calm and peaceful shall I sleep,
Rocked in the cradle of the deep.

NATHANIEL P. WILLIS

1806—1867

TWO WOMEN

The shadows lay along Broadway,
  'Twas near the twilight tide,
And slowly there a lady fair
  Was walking in her pride—
Alone walked she, yet viewlessly
  Walked spirits at her side.

Peace charmed the street beneath her feet,
  And Honor charmed the air;
And all astir looked kind on her,
  And called her good as fair;—

For all God ever gave to her
  She kept with chary care.

She kept with care her beauties rare
  From lovers warm and true;
For her heart was cold to all but gold,
  And the rich came not to woo:—
Ah, honored well are charms to sell,
  If priests the selling do.

Now, walking there was one more fair—
  A slight girl, lily-pale;
And she had unseen company
  To make the spirit quail:
'Twixt want and scorn she walked forlorn,
  And nothing could avail.

No mercy now can clear her brow
  For this world's peace to pray;
For, as love's wild prayer dissolved in air,
  Her woman's heart gave way!—
And the sin forgiven by Christ in heaven
  By man is cursed alway!

FORCEYTHE WILLSON

1837—1867

THE OLD SERGEANT

"Come a little nearer, Doctor,—thank you,—let me take the cup:
Draw your chair up,—draw it closer,—just another little sup!

May be you may think I'm better; but I'm pretty
well used up:—
Doctor, you've done all you could do, but I'm
just a going up!
"Feel my pulse, sir, if you want to, but it ain't much
use to try:"—
"Never say that," said the Surgeon as he smothered
down a sigh;
"It will never do, old comrade, for a soldier to say
die!"
"What you *say* will make no difference, Doctor,
when you come to die.

"Doctor, what has been the matter?" "You were
very faint, they say;
You must try to get to sleep now." "Doctor, have
I been away?"
"Not that anybody knows of!" "Doctor—Doctor,
please to stay!
There is something I must tell you, and you won't
have long to stay!

"I have got my marching orders, and I'm ready now
to go;
Doctor, did you say I fainted?—but it couldn't ha'
been so,—
For as sure as I'm a sergeant, and was wounded at
Shiloh,
I've this very night been back there, on the old
field of Shiloh!

"This is all that I remember: the last time the
Lighter came,
And the lights had all been lowered, and the noises
much the same,

He had not been gone five minutes before something called my name:
'Orderly Sergeant—Robert Burton!'—just that way it called my name.

"And I wondered who could call me so distinctly and so slow,
Knew it couldn't be the Lighter,—he could not have spoken so,—
And I tried to answer, 'Here, sir!' but I couldn't make it go;
For I couldn't move a muscle, and I couldn't make it go!

"Then I thought: it's all a nightmare, all a humbug and a bore;
Just another foolish grape-vine,—and it won't come any more;
But it came, sir, notwithstanding, just the same way as before:
'Orderly Sergeant—Robert Burton!'—even plainer than before.

"That is all that I remember, till a sudden burst of light,
And I stood beside the river, where we stood that Sunday night,
Waiting to be ferried over to the dark bluffs opposite,
When the river was perdition and all hell was opposite!—

"And the same old palpitation came again in all its power,
And I heard a Bugle sounding, as from some celestial Tower;

And the same mysterious voice said: 'IT IS THE
ELEVENTH HOUR!
ORDERLY SERGEANT—ROBERT BURTON—IT IS THE
ELEVENTH HOUR!'

"Doctor Austin!—what *day* is this?" "It is Wednesday night, you know."
"Yes,—to-morrow will be New Year's and a right
good time below!
What *time* is it, Doctor Austin?" "Nearly Twelve."
"Then don't you go!
Can it be that all this happened—all this—not an
hour ago!

"There was where the gunboats opened on the dark
rebellious host;
And where Webster semicircled his last guns upon
the coast;
There were still the two log-houses, just the same, or
else their ghost,—
And the same old transport came and took me
over—or its ghost!

"And the old field lay before me all deserted far
and wide;
There was where they fell on Prentiss,—there McClernand met the tide;
There was where stern Sherman rallied, and where
Hurlbut's heroes died,—
Lower down, where Wallace charged them, and
kept charging till he died.

"There was where Lew Wallace showed them he was of the canny kin,
There was where old Nelson thundered, and where Rousseau waded in;
There McCook sent 'em to breakfast, and we all began to win—
There was where the grape-shot took me, just as we began to win.

"Now, a shroud of snow and silence over everything was spread;
And but for this old blue mantle and the old hat on my head,
I should not have even doubted, to this moment, I was dead,—
For my footsteps were as silent as the snow upon the dead!

"Death and silence!—Death and silence! all around me as I sped!
And, behold, a mighty Tower, as if builded to the dead,
To the Heaven of the heavens lifted up its mighty head,
Till the Stars and Stripes of Heaven all seemed waving from its head!

"Round and mighty-based it towered—up into the infinite—
And I knew no mortal mason could have built a shaft so bright;
For it shone like solid sunshine; and a winding stair of light
Wound around it and around it till it wound clear out of sight!

"And, behold, as I approached it,—with a rapt and dazzled stare,—
Thinking that I saw old comrades just ascending the great Stair,—
Suddenly the solemn challenge broke of, 'Halt, and who goes there!'
'I'm a friend,' I said, 'if you are.' 'Then advance, sir, to the Stair!'
"I advanced!—That sentry, Doctor, was Elijah Ballantyne!—
First of all to fall on Monday, after we had formed the line!—
'Welcome, my old Sergeant, welcome! welcome by that countersign!'
And he pointed to the scar there, under this old cloak of mine!

"As he grasped my hand, I shuddered, thinking only of the grave;
But he smiled and pointed upward with a bright and bloodless glaive:
'That's the way, sir, to Headquarters.' 'What Headquarters?' 'Of the Brave.'
'But the great Tower?' 'That,' he answered, 'is the way, sir, of the Brave!'
"Then a sudden shame came o'er me at his uniform of light;
At my own so old and tattered, and at his so new and bright:
'Ah!' said he, 'you have forgotten the New Uniform to-night,—
Hurry back, for you must be here at just twelve o'clock to-night!'

"And the next thing I remember, you were sitting
there, and I—
Doctor—did you hear a footstep? Hark!—God bless
you all! Good by!
Doctor, please to give my musket and my knapsack,
when I die,
To my son—my son that's coming,—he won't get
here till I die!

"Tell him his old father blessed him as he never
did before,—
And to carry that old musket—hark! a knock is at
the door!—
Till the Union— See! it opens!" "Father! father!
speak once more!"
"*Bless you!*" gasped the old, gray Sergeant, and he
lay and said no more!

JOHN WILMOT, EARL OF ROCHESTER

1647—1680

ON CHARLES II

HERE lies our Sovereign Lord the King,
Whose word no man relies on,
Who never said a foolish thing,
Nor ever did a wise one.

HORATIO WINSLOW

1882—

HERE'S THE END OF DREAMLAND

HERE'S the end of Dreamland, here's the Road of
Day;
Kiss me of your kindness and let me go my way.

All the hours we squandered, all the miles we went,
They were the gold of Dreamland and all the gold is spent.

Hard and hard, O heart of Me, overhard it seems:—
Lord! the pleasant palaces . . . in the Land of Dreams.

GEORGE WITHER

1588—1667

THE MANLY HEART

SHALL I, wasting in despair,
Die because a woman's fair?
Or make pale my cheeks with care
'Cause another's rosy are?
Be she fairer than the day
Or the flowery meads in May—
If she think not well of me
What care I how fair she be?

Shall my silly heart be pined
'Cause I see a woman kind;
Or a well disposéd nature
Joinéd with a lovely feature?
Be she meeker, kinder, than
Turtle-dove or pelican,
If she be not so to me
What care I how kind she be?

Shall a woman's virtues move
Me to perish for her love?
Or her well-deservings known
Make me quite forget mine own?

Be she with that goodness blest
Which may merit name of Best;
If she be not such to me,
What care I how good she be?

'Cause her fortune seems too high,
Shall I play the fool and die?
She that bears a noble mind,
If not outward helps she find,
Thinks what with them he would do
Who without them dares her woo;
And unless that mind I see,
What care I how great she be?

Great or good, or kind, or fair,
I will ne'er the more despair;
If she love me, this believe,
I will die ere she shall grieve;
If she slight me when I woo,
I can scorn and let her go;
For if she be not for me,
What care I for whom she be?

C. WOLFE

1791—1823

THE BURIAL OF SIR JOHN MOORE AT CORUNNA

NOT a drum was heard, not a funeral note,
As his corpse to the rampart we hurried;
Not a soldier discharged his farewell shot
O'er the grave where our hero we buried.

C. WOLFE

We buried him darkly at the dead of night,
  The sods with our bayonets turning;
By the struggling moonbeam's misty light
  And the lantern dimly burning.

No useless coffin enclosed his breast,
  Not in sheet or in shroud we wound him;
But he lay like a warrior taking his rest,
  With his martial cloak around him.

Few and short were the prayers we said,
  And we spoke not a word of sorrow;
But we steadfastly gazed on the face that was dead,
  And we bitterly thought of the morrow.

We thought, as we hollow'd his narrow bed
  And smoothed down his lonely pillow,
That the foe and the stranger would tread o'er his head,
  And we far away on the billow!

Lightly they'll talk of the spirit that's gone
  And o'er his cold ashes upbraid him,—
But little he'll reck, if they let him sleep on
  In the grave where a Briton has laid him.

But half of our heavy task was done
  When the clock struck the hour for retiring:
And we heard the distant and random gun
  That the foe was sullenly firing.

Slowly and sadly we laid him down,
  From the field of his fame fresh and gory;
We carved not a line, and we raised not a stone,
  But we left him alone with his glory.

CLEMENT WOOD

1888—

DE GLORY ROAD

O DE Glory Road! O de Glory Road!
I'm gwine ter drap mah load upon de Glory Road.

I lay on mah bed untell one erclock,
An' de Lawd come callin' all His faithful flock.
An' He call "Whoo-ee!", an' He call "Whoo-ee!"
An' I knowed dat de Sabior wuz ercallin' me.
An' He call "Whoo-ee!", an' He call "Whoo-ee!",
An' I cry, "Massa Jesus, is you callin' me?"
An' He call "Whoo-ee!", an' He call "Whoo-ee!",
An' I riz up f'um mah pallet, an' I cry, "Hyahs me!"

De Lawd sez, "Niggah, ain' I call yer thrice
'Ter ride erlong behin' me up ter Paradise,
On de Glory Road, on de Glory Road?"
An' I clime up ter de saddle, an' I jined de load!

De hawse he wuz longer dan a thousan' mile';
His tail went lashin', an' his hoofs wuz wil';
His mane wuz flamin', an' his eyes wuz moons,
An' his mouth kep' singin' Halleluyah tunes!

De Lawd sez, "Niggah, why 'n' cher look erroun'?"
An' dar we wuz flyin' over risin' groun'.
Powerful hills, an' mountains too,
An' de earth an' de people wuz drapt f'um view.

An' I hyahd all 'roun' me how de sperits sang,
An' de Lawd sang louder dan de whole shebang!

De Lawd sez, "Niggah, why n'n cher look ergin?"
An' dar wuz de Debbil, on de back uv Sin,

A-bangin' on de critter wid his whip an' goad,
An' boun' he gwine ter kotch us, on de Glory Road!
"O Lawdy, it's de Debbil, comin' straight f'um
Hell!
I kin tell him by his roarin', an' de brimstone smell!"
But de Lawd sez, "Niggah, he ain' kotch us yit!"
An' He lashed an' He hustled, an' He loosed de bit.
Den de Debbil crep' closuh, an' I hyahd him yell,
"I'm gwine ter kotch a niggah, fur ter roas' in Hell!"
An' I cried, "Lawd, sabe me!" An' de Lawd cry,
"Sho!"
An' hyah it was Hebben, an' we shet de do'.

O Glory, Glory, how de angels sang!
O Glory, O Glory, how de rafters rang!
An' Moses 'n' Aaron, an' Methusalum,
Dey shout an' dey holler, an' dey beat de drum.
King Solomon kissed me, an' his thousan' wives,
Jes' like dey'd knowed me, durin' all dey lives;
An' de Lawd sez, "Niggah, take a gran'-stan' seat.
But I 'specks youse hongry; have a bite ter eat?"
An' de ravens fed me, an' Elijah prayed,
An' de Sabed Ones gathered, while de organ played,
An' dey cry, "O sinnah, come an' lose yuh load
On de Glory Road, on de Glory Road.
An' come an' dwell in de Lawd's abode,
Glory, Glory, on de Glory Road!"

Sez de Lawd, "No, sinnah, you mus' trabbel back
Ter he'p po' niggahs up de Glory Track;

Ter he'p old mo'ners, an' de scoffin' coons,
By shoutin' loud Halleluyah tunes."

O come, mah breddren, won' you drap yuh load,
An' ride ter Hebben up de Glory Road?

WILLIAM WORDSWORTH

1770—1850

SHE WAS A PHANTOM OF DELIGHT

SHE was a Phantom of delight
When first she gleam'd upon my sight;
A lovely Apparition, sent
To be a moment's ornament;
Her eyes as stars of Twilight fair;
Like Twilight's, too, her dusky hair;
But all things else about her drawn
From May-time and the cheerful Dawn;
A dancing Shape, an Image gay,
To haunt, to startle, and waylay.

I saw her upon nearer view,
A Spirit, yet a Woman too!
Her household motions light and free,
And steps of virgin liberty;
A countenance in which did meet
Sweet records, promises as sweet;
A Creature not too bright or good
For human nature's daily food;
For transient sorrows, simple wiles,
Praise, blame, love, kisses, tears, and smiles.

And now I see with eye serene
The very pulse of the machine;

A Being breathing thoughtful breath,
A Traveller between life and death;
The reason firm, the temperate will,
Endurance, foresight, strength, and skill;
A perfect Woman, nobly plann'd,
To warn, to comfort, and command;
And yet a Spirit still, and bright
With something of angelic light.

LUCY

She dwelt among the untrodden ways
  Beside the springs of Dove,
A maid whom there were none to praise,
  And very few to love.

A violet by a mossy stone
  Half-hidden from the eye!
—Fair as a star, when only one
  Is shining in the sky.

She lived unknown, and few could know
  When Lucy ceased to be;
But she is in her grave, and, oh,
  The difference to me!

ENGLAND AND SWITZERLAND, 1802

Two Voices are there; one is of the Sea,
One of the Mountains; each a mighty voice:
In both from age to age thou didst rejoice,
They were thy chosen music, Liberty!

There came a tyrant, and with holy glee
Thou fought'st against him,—but hast vainly striven:
Thou from thy Alpine holds at length art driven,
Where not a torrent murmurs heard by thee.

—Of one deep bliss thine ear hath been bereft;
Then cleave, O cleave to that which still is left—
For, high-soul'd Maid, what sorrow would it be

That Mountain floods should thunder as before,
And Ocean bellow from his rocky shore,
And neither awful Voice be heard by Thee!

ODE TO DUTY

STERN Daughter of the Voice of God!
O Duty! if that name thou love
Who art a light to guide, a rod
To check the erring, and reprove;
Thou who are victory and law
When empty terrors overawe;
From vain temptations dost set free,
And calm'st the weary strife of frail humanity!

There are who ask not if thine eye
Be on them; who, in love and truth
Where no misgiving is, rely
Upon the genial sense of youth:
Glad hearts! without reproach or blot,
Who do thy work, and know it not:
Oh! if through confidence misplaced
They fail, thy saving arms, dread Power! around them cast.

Serene will be our days and bright
And happy will our nature be,
When love is an unerring light,
And joy its own security.
And they a blissful course may hold
Ev'n now, who, not unwisely bold,
Live in the spirit of this creed;
Yet seek thy firm support, according to their need.

I, loving freedom, and untried,
No sport of every random gust,
Yet being to myself a guide,
Too blindly have reposed my trust:
And oft, when in my heart was heard
Thy timely mandate, I deferr'd
The task, in smoother walks to stray;
But thee I now would serve more strictly, if I may.

Through no disturbance of my soul
Or strong compunction in me wrought,
I supplicate for thy control,
But in the quietness of thought:
Me this uncharter'd freedom tires;
I feel the weight of chance desires:
My hopes no more must change their name;
I long for a repose that ever is the same.

Stern Lawgiver! yet thou dost wear
The Godhead's most benignant grace;
Nor know we anything so fair
As is the smile upon thy face:

Flowers laugh before thee on their beds,
And fragrance in thy footing treads;
Thou dost preserve the stars from wrong;
And the most ancient heavens, through thee, are fresh and strong.

TO THE CUCKOO

O BLITHE new-comer! I have heard,
I hear thee and rejoice:
O Cuckoo! shall I call thee Bird,
Or but a wandering Voice?

While I am lying on the grass
Thy twofold shout I hear;
From hill to hill it seems to pass,
At once far off and near.

Though babbling only to the vale
Of sunshine and of flowers,
Thou bringest unto me a tale
Of visionary hours.

Thrice welcome, darling of the Spring!
Even yet thou art to me
No bird, but an invisible thing,
A voice, a mystery;

The same whom in my school-boy days
I listen'd to; that Cry
Which made me look a thousand ways
In bush, and tree, and sky.

To seek thee did I often rove
Through woods and on the green;
And thou wert still a hope, a love;
Still long'd for, never seen!

And I can listen to thee yet;
Can lie upon the plain
And listen, till I do beget
That golden time again.

O blesséd Bird! the earth we pace
Again appears to be
An unsubstantial, faery place,
That is fit home for Thee!

THE WORLD IS TOO MUCH WITH US

THE World is too much with us; late and soon,
Getting and spending, we lay waste our powers;
Little we see in Nature that is ours;
We have given our hearts away, a sordid boon!

This Sea that bares her bosom to the moon,
The winds that will be howling at all hours
And are up-gather'd now like sleeping flowers,
For this, for every thing, we are out of tune;

It moves us not.—Great God! I'd rather be
A Pagan suckled in a creed outwarn.—
So might I, standing on this pleasant lea,

Have glimpses that would make me less forlorn;
Have sight of Proteus rising from the sea;
Or hear Old Triton blow his wreathéd horn.

THE DAFFODILS

I WANDER'D lonely as a cloud
That floats on high o'er vales and hills,
When all at once I saw a crowd,
A host of golden daffodils,
Beside the lake, beneath the trees,
Fluttering and dancing in the breeze.

Continuous as the stars that shine
And twinkle on the milky way,
They stretch'd in never-ending line
Along the margin of a bay:
Ten thousand saw I at a glance
Tossing their heads in sprightly dance.

The waves beside them danced, but they
Out-did the sparkling waves in glee:—
A Poet could not but be gay
In such a jocund company!
I gazed—and gazed—but little thought
What wealth the show to me had brought;

For oft, when on my couch I lie
In vacant or in pensive mood,
They flash upon that inward eye
Which is the bliss of solitude;
And then my heart with pleasure fills,
And dances with the daffodils.

ODE ON INTIMATIONS OF IMMORTALITY FROM RECOLLECTIONS OF EARLY CHILDHOOD

THERE was a time when meadow, grove, and stream
The earth, and every common sight
To me did seem
Apparell'd in celestial light,
The glory and the freshness of a dream.
It is not now as it hath been of yore;—
Turn wheresoe'er I may,
By night or day,
The things which I have seen I now can see no more.
The rainbow comes and goes,
And lovely is the rose;
The moon doth with delight
Look round her when the heavens are bare;
Waters on a starry night
Are beautiful and fair;
The sunshine is a glorious birth;
But yet I know, where'er I go,
That there hath past away a glory from the earth.
Now, while the birds thus sing a joyous song,
And while the young lambs bound
As to the tabor's sound,
To me alone there came a thought of grief:
A timely utterance gave that thought relief,
And I again am strong:
The cataracts blow their trumpets from the steep;
No more shall grief of mine the season wrong;
I hear the echoes through the mountains throng,
The winds come to me from the fields of sleep,

And all the earth is gay;
Land and sea
Give themselves up to jollity,
And with the heart of May
Doth every beast keep holiday;—
Thou Child of Joy,
Shout round me, let me hear thy shouts, thou happy
Shepherd-boy!

Ye blessèd Creatures, I have heard the call
Ye to each other make; I see
The heavens laugh with you in your jubilee;
My heart is at your festival,
My head hath its coronal,
The fulness of your bliss, I feel—I feel it all.
Oh evil day! If I were sullen
While Earth herself is adorning
This sweet May-morning,
And the children are culling
On every side
In a thousand valleys far and wide,
Fresh flowers; while the sun shines warm
And the babe leaps up on his mother's arm:—
I hear, I hear, with joy I hear!
—But there's a tree, of many, one,
A single field which I have look'd upon,
Both of them speak of something that is gone:
The pansy at my feet
Doth the same tale repeat:
Whither is fled the visionary gleam?
Where is it now, the glory and the dream?

Our birth is but a sleep and a forgetting;
The Soul that rises with us, our life's Star,

Hath had elsewhere its setting
And cometh from afar;
Not in entire forgetfulness,
And not in utter nakedness.
But trailing clouds of glory do we come
From God, who is our home:
Heaven lies about us in our infancy!
Shades of the prison-house begin to close
Upon the growing Boy,
But he beholds the light, and whence it flows,
He sees it in his joy;
The Youth, who daily farther from the east
Must travel, still is Nature's priest,
And by the vision splendid
Is on his way attended;
At length the Man perceives it die away,
And fade into the light of common day.

Earth fills her lap with pleasures of her own;
Yearnings she hath in her own natural kind,
And, even with something of a mother's mind
And no unworthy aim,
The homely nurse doth all she can
To make her foster-child, her inmate, Man,
Forget the glories he hath known,
And that imperial palace whence he came.

Behold the Child among his new-born blisses,
A six years' darling of a pigmy size!
See, where 'mid work of his own hand he lies,
Fretted by sallies of his mother's kisses,
With light upon him from his father's eyes!
See, at his feet, some little plan or chart,

Some fragment from his dream of human life,
Shaped by himself with newly-learnèd art;
A wedding or a festival,
A mourning or a funeral;
And this hath now his heart,
And unto this he frames his song:
Then will he fit his tongue
To dialogues of business, love, or strife;
But it will not be long,
Ere this be thrown aside,
And with new joy and pride
The little actor cons another part;
Filling from time to time his 'humorous stage'
With all the Persons, down to palsied Age,
That life brings with her in her equipage;
As if his whole vocation
Were endless imitation.

Thou, whose exterior semblance doth belie
Thy soul's immensity;
Thou best Philosopher, who yet dost keep
Thy heritage, thou Eye among the blind,
That, deaf and silent, read'st the eternal deep,
Haunted for ever by the eternal Mind,—
Mighty Prophet? Seer blest!
On whom those truths do rest,
Which we are toiling all our lives to find,
In darkness lost, the darkness of the grave;
Thou, over whom thy Immortaility
Broods like the Day, a Master o'er a Slave,
A Presence which is not to be put by;
Why with such earnest pains doth thou provoke
The years to bring the inevitable yoke,

Thus blindly with thy blessedness at strife?
Full soon thy soul shall have her earthly freight,
And custom lie upon thee with a weight
Heavy as frost, and deep almost as life!

O joy! that in our embers
Is something that doth live,
That Nature yet remembers
What was so fugitive!
The thought of our past years in me doth breed
Perpetual benediction: not indeed
For that which is most worthy to be blest,
Delight and liberty, the simple creed
Of childhood, whether busy or at rest.
With new-fledged hope still fluttering in his breast:—
—Not for these I raise
The songs of thanks and praise;
But for those obstinate questionings
Of sense and outward things,
Fallings from us, vanishings;
Blank misgivings of a creature
Moving about in worlds not realized,
High instincts, before which our mortal nature
Did tremble like a guilty thing surprized:
But for those first affections,
Those shadowy recollections,
Which, be they what they may,
Are yet the fountain light of all our day,
Are yet a master-light of all our seeing;
Uphold us, cherish, and have power to make
Our noisy years seem moments in the being
Of the eternal Silence: truths that wake,
To perish never;

Which neither listlessness, nor mad endeavor,
Nor man nor boy
Nor all that is at enmity with joy,
Can utterly abolish or destroy!

Yet in my heart of hearts I feel your might;
I only have relinquish'd one delight
To live beneath your more habitual sway.
I love the Brooks which down their channels fret,
Even more than when I tripp'd lightly as they;
The innocent brightness of a new-born Day
Is lovely yet;
The Clouds that gather round the setting sun
Do take a sober colouring from any eye
That hath kept watch o'er man's mortality;
Another race hath been, and other palms are won.
Thanks to the human heart by which we live,
Thanks to its tenderness, its joys, and fears,
To me the meanest flower that blows can give
Thoughts that do often lie too deep for tears.

William Wadsworth

MILTON

MILTON! thou shouldst be living at this hour:
England hath need of thee: she is a fen
Of stagnant waters: altar, sword, and pen,
Fireside, the heroic wealth of hall and bower,

Have forfeited their ancient English dower
Of inward happiness. We are selfish men:
Oh! raise us up, return to us again;
And give us manners, virtue, freedom, power.

Thy soul was like a Star, and dwelt apart:
Thou hadst a voice whose sound was like the sea,
Pure as the naked heavens, majestic, free;
So didst thou travel on life's common way
In cheerful godliness; and yet thy heart
The lowliest duties on herself did lay.

SIR T. WYAT

1503—1542

A SUPPLICATION

Forget not yet the tried intent
Of such a truth as I have meant;
My great travail so gladly spent,
Forget not yet!

Forget not yet when first began
The weary life ye know, since whan
The suit, the service none tell can;
Forget not yet!

Forget not yet the great assays,
The cruel wrong, the scornful ways,
The painful patience in delays,
Forget not yet!

Forget not! O, forget not this,
How long ago hath been, and is
The mind that never meant amiss—
Forget not yet!

Forget not then thine own approved
The which so long hath thee so loved,
Whose steadfast faith yet never moved—
Forget not this!

THE LOVER'S APPEAL

AND wilt thou leave me thus!
Say nay, say nay, for shame!
To save thee from the blame
Of all my grief and grame.
And wilt thou leave me thus?
Say nay! say nay!

And wilt thou leave me thus,
That hath loved thee so long
In wealth and woe among:
And is thy heart so strong
As for to leave me thus?
Say nay! say nay!

And wilt thou leave me thus,
That hath given thee my heart
Never for to depart
Neither for pain nor smart:
And wilt thou leave me thus?
Say nay! say nay!

And wilt thou leave me thus,
And have no more pity
Of him that loveth thee?
Alas! thy cruelty
And wilt thou leave me thus?
Say nay! say nay!